Making the most of EASTER

Contents

Preparing for Lent

Many people are not even aware of the name 'Lent'. It is worth using church notices, magazine articles, and sermons to outline its:

- ❑ origins – as baptism instruction and preparation for Easter
- ❑ opportunities – for individuals and churches to take stock
- ❑ importance – as part of the rhythm of church life
- ❑ themes – of sin, changing direction, guidance, abstinence, commitment
- ❑ fasting and feasting – Lent's forty weekdays of fasting and six Sundays of feasting offer a chance to emphasize these aspects of Christian living.

Shrove Tuesday

Shrove Tuesday (or the Saturday before) is an opportunity for all the church family to get together. Try a pancake party with, perhaps, the children doing the serving. Have pancake races for different age groups. Or have 'A mad hatter's tea party' encouraging everyone to come with an extravagant hat! Older people and children will love this.

Make it one of the 'feasting' occasions. Make sure it's fun and tries to meet an identifiable need.

Picking up the themes of God's goodness and of the joy in serving him will provide a helpful lead into Lent. An introduction to home group or sermon themes can be launched at this event.

Ash Wednesday

You need to decide how important Ash Wednesday is in your church's plans for Lent and Easter.

If the church is going through a difficult time, the Ashing Service, adapted from the book *Lent, Holy Week and Easter* (SPCK), can be used to good effect. It can draw attention to the need for corporate confession of wrong and submission to God. Careful preparation is needed, and rehearsal of the practical detail will be important.

If the church is about to enter a new phase of its life, Ash Wednesday is a good time to seek God's blessing upon it. The announcement of a new programme or a special initiative, or a series of teaching themes, can all be launched from the natural platform of Ash Wednesday.

Ash Wednesday can also be used as a time for seeking God's will and purposes for the church as it faces some problem or opportunity, or for focusing on some special need within the church or wider community. Some churches make a point of using this time to initiate and complete some social project in the area or to raise money for some cause further afield.

There are churches where it will be impossible to make much use of Ash Wednesday because of people's work patterns. In this case either the Sunday before or after can be used. It is important to realize, however, that this time of the church's year is just waiting to be exploited!

Lent meals

It may be helpful to lay on a Ploughman's Lunch on a regular day each week in Lent. Many, especially those not in employment, may welcome this. Make it an ecumenical venture or maybe target it for a section of the community. Alternatively, you could hold an early morning prayer time and combine it with breakfast.

Prayer

Many people are aware of their need of help where prayer is concerned. Apart from teaching series, practical help can be given about private prayer, praying in groups and making the best use of prayer times in church services. Those new to praying can be encouraged to write out one-line prayers, or be helped to turn conversation with others into prayers.

The Lord's Prayer is a helpful model to teach from and to encourage people to use.

Teaching series

The six Sundays (the six 'feasting' days as against the forty 'fasting' days of Lent) are ideal opportunities for teaching. The content can be related to *Alternative Service Book* themes, to the cross, to a Bible book, or to many others. It can also focus upon individuals' own encounters with God and their growth in faith.

Collages, mosaics or banners, and church decoration, drama, or home group contributions can all be used to reinforce the teaching and make it more easily remembered.

In order to give focus to Lent, one church invited the children to go looking for cards which had been placed all round the church, with 'Alleluia' marked on them. They then brought them forward to the sound of the 'Hallelujah Chorus' and put them in a large box (with the fun of one or two falling outside and the music starting up again!). The box was to be reopened at Easter. It was explained that the emphasis in Lent was not going to be on praise but on the church's need to examine itself and consider with an extra degree of seriousness some important issues which were before it.

Longings

Lord, you know the ache that burns inside me,
You know about the longings of my soul.
Lord, you know I need your strength and Shoulders
To carry me, to keep this body whole.

If it weren't for you I know my life would fall Apart.
If it weren't for you the cracks would start to Show.
But you lift me and refuse to let me Crumble –
Though I often slam the door on you and go.

I often leave and walk away defeated,
Empty from the dreary days ahead.
Thank you that you never let me go –
But you bind my wounds, and heal my heart,
And tell me that you love me once again.

MOTHERING SUNDAY

Take care!

Be careful to ensure that the importance of the role of other adults and especially that of single women is not neglected on Mothering Sunday. Emphasizing the value of the role of mothers is crucially important, but if it is to the exclusion of others, it will be unhelpful.

Flowers

If flowers are to be prepared and given, make sure that all women receive a bunch. Flowers can be prepared by children the day before. Preparation for other gifts can be included in children's groups' work in the week or weeks beforehand.

Family service talk: A word from a flower

Jesus used flowers to illustrate a point about trust in God. This talk uses a flower to speak about what we want to say to our mothers and what God wants to say to us.

Matthew 6:28

Visual aids:	*On OHP slides make up a flower, petal by petal, with the centre being added last*

The petals can say:

- ❑ **I'm thinking of you.** We send flowers to people when we are thinking of them. Today is the day when we think of mothers. But God is always thinking of us (Psalm 139).
- ❑ **You love me.** Flowers often convey a message when given to someone. As we give flowers to our mothers, we know that they love us. God loves us too (John 3:16).
- ❑ **You are special.** Flowers often say this, too. We say today to our mothers that they are special to us and we thank them that we are special to them. God sees us all as special and unique people (1 Peter 2:9; Psalm 17:8). But do we really make God special in our lives?
- ❑ **Thank you.** Saying 'thank you' is very important. We say it especially today. God's people should always say 'thank you' to God (Psalm 138).
- ❑ **When I consider all you have done.** Today is a chance to think about all the things mothers do for us. It is also a chance to think about what God has done for us (Psalm 8).

❏ **I love you.** We say it with flowers but also with our lips and hearts. God wants us to do the same to him (John 14:21; Psalm 18:1).

Family service talk: A family in need
2 Kings 4:1-7

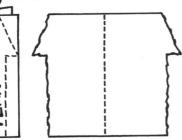

Use this story to illustrate God's care through his servant, Elisha, for a family in great need.

Visual aids:	OHP slides

Not all families are the same. Some mums and dads have many children, some have none, and some children have only one parent. This family had a mum and two sons and was in great need.

❏ **God loves all families.** God's prophet comes and helps (verse 2). We need to help ourselves but also to help one another.
❏ **God expects young and old to work together** (verse 4).
❏ **God brought about a wonderful change** (verse 7). He can do that for us whatever our situation.

Family service talk: Togetherness

Visual aids:	Large sheet of stiff paper, torn as shown

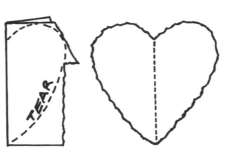 

LIVING   LOVING   LISTENING

Luke 2:51-52

❏ **Living in a family.** While he was a child, Jesus lived with his parents. Later on he lived alone or with companions in their and others' homes. Both were important to his ministry. Family and single life have advantages and disadvantages.
❏ **Loving in a family.** A loving family is vitally important for everybody. So much of what we will be like as adults depends on what happens in our early years at home.
❏ **Listening in a family.** Jesus had to explain to his parents what he was doing. Talking and listening is important for all, young to old and old to young (Ephesians 6:1-4).

Reading: Neville and Toad

Neville the Frog had forgotten again. He always forgot. Today was Mother's Day and Neville had forgotten to send the card. Actually, it wasn't really a card, it was an old Mars Bar wrapper and of course it didn't say 'Happy Mother's Day', it said 'Official food of the Olympic team' but his mother would understand. She always understood his messages. He was never very good at things like this. He couldn't really make anything because he always fumbled and dropped it in the river, and even an old Mars Bar wrapper is better than a soggy present. Except this year his mother wouldn't even get the wrapper. He had forgotten again. Neville sighed and shook his head. He knew what he must do.

Toad tapped his fingers together and thought for a while. Neville gulped nervously. He was now sitting in Toad's front room. Wise Toad who knew everything. Neville was sure he would know the answer.

'I could post it today first class and pretend that it was all the post office's fault!' Neville suggested. Toad shook his head.

'Well, I could just not bother at all – forget all about it.' Toad shook his head again.

Neville had run out of ideas now and he was beginning to feel very uncomfortable. He could only ever store two good ideas inside his little head. There simply wasn't room for any more.

Toad suddenly sat up very straight. 'I've got it!' he said. 'Go and see her!'

Neville's mouth dropped open. 'Go and see her? But, but... she lives miles away and it'll take ages and ages and ages to hop there. At least twenty minutes!'

'Good,' said Toad, 'it'll help you keep fit. And you can pick some flowers on the way. Hopping's very good for you, you know.'

Neville didn't seem so sure. 'I've already hopped today. I hopped for a whole ten minutes to come to your house,' he said.

Toad smiled his knowing smile. 'Just think,' he said, 'if you go to see your mother yourself imagine the surprise on her face when she opens the door. Not only that – but then you could give the Mars Bar wrapper to her right on time!'

Neville nodded slowly and looked thoughtful. 'It isn't always easy to sort out a problem, is it?' he said.

'No,' said Toad, 'the answer to a problem isn't always the easiest thing to do. But it is still the answer.'

And with that thought in his head, Neville stood up, flexed his little legs, and began the long twenty-minute hop to his mother's lily pad.

Reading: Abraham and Sarah

During this reading, people join in with the following responses:

Stars – All look up and shield eyes with hand
Cows – All go: 'Moo!'
Dogs – All go: 'Woof!'
Baby – All cry
Sand – All rub hands
Laughed – All laugh

A long time ago there was a man called Abraham. He had a wife called Sarah, and lots and lots of animals. Every night Abraham would stand outside and look up at the sky trying to count the **stars**. He would sit on the **sand**, with his **dogs**, and his **cows**. And one night as he was out there with the **stars** and the **sand** and the **dogs** and the **cows** – all of a sudden God appeared and said, 'Abraham – your wife is going to have a **baby**!'

Well, Abraham was so surprised he nearly **laughed** because he and Sarah were very old and it was a shock to think they might have a **baby**. But the Lord told him that nothing is impossible for God to do and that Abraham and Sarah would have so many relatives that they wouldn't be able to count them all.

In fact this one **baby** would become a great nation of people – more than all the **stars**, more than the grains of **sand**, and more than all the **dogs** and **cows**.

Well, Abraham thought about this for a long time – in fact, he thought about it every night as he sat out with the **stars** and the **sand** and the **dogs** and the **cows**. And sometimes he got quite excited about it. But a long, long time went by and they still didn't have a **baby**.

Then three visitors came to see him. And while they ate some tea, they said that quite soon Sarah would be a mother. When Sarah heard this she **laughed**... and **laughed**... and **laughed** – but sure enough a year later she had a **baby**!

And from then on, every time they sat outside Abraham looked at the **stars**, and the **sand** and the **dogs** and the **cows**, and he remembered God's promise that one day he and Sarah would be the parents of a great nation.

From a son

Mothers.
Boy, do we need them.
They always come up with the goods.
That missing sock under the bed, the rushed breakfast munched in the doorway; the crisp washing and clean sheets; the hot meal still waiting after three hours of rugby practice.

Yes – mothers do come in very handy.
They're useful – helpful – loving – and generous.

They really serve a purpose.

At least that's the way I see it.
But I suppose there is actually a person inside my mother. A free thinking individual.

I almost forgot.

She was such a necessity – a support, a shoulder... a servant.
But I suppose mothers are real people, with mothers of their own.
Needing their own mothers just as I need mine.

Needing a help – a support, a shoulder... a servant.

What! *Me* serve my own mother! Now, that's a bit of a shock. I can give her breakfast on Mother's Day, even take that embarrassing walk to collect the flowers at the front of the church in the family service.

But serve my own mother?
Now, that's a bit radical.

I think tea in bed is much safer.

HOLY WEEK: INTRODUCTION

Sticking to a theme

Arrange a programme for your church which emphasizes one particular theme throughout the whole of Holy Week. Examples could be:

- ❑ **Jerusalem journey.** A geographical survey of 'what happened where' during Holy Week. Make good use of visual materials such as slides, maps, videos and overhead projectors.
- ❑ **Characters at the cross.** Concentrate on a particular character each day, seeing events through that person's eyes. Examples could be: a member of the crowd, one of the disciples, one of the women, Simon of Cyrene, the centurion, Barabbas, the criminals.
- ❑ **Power and powerlessness.** Who were those who had power? How was it exercised? Where did real power lie? What is the relationship between power and powerlessness for the Christian?

Using the senses

There are significant changes of mood and emotion in the Gospel accounts of Palm Sunday and the Passion. Try to develop some of these moods and emotions in your services by imaginatively incorporating the use of all the senses: sight, sound, touch, smell, taste. Enable people to experience the feelings of being in a noisy crowd; having a meal with friends; feeling tired, and praying in a dark garden; being left wondering what was going on for three days from Good Friday to Easter Sunday; perhaps even being betrayed. This will have more impact than a traditional reiteration of the facts alone.

Procession	Many churches start their Palm Sunday with a procession, setting off from a location in the local community (e.g. school car park, market square), and ending in the church, which acts as the temple at Jerusalem. Music and chanting (in Graham Kendrick's 'Make Way' style) accompany the procession. Ensure co-operation with local police if the procession is outside church premises.
Use of visual materials	Slides of Jerusalem from the Mount of Olives help to understand how it felt to see Jerusalem. Some photocopying shops are able to copy slides on to overhead projector acetates if blackout is a problem. Maps, photographs and pictures in books can also be photocopied directly on to acetates. A series of excellent slide programmes, videos, maps, etc. can be obtained from Biblical Resources, PO Box 19556, Jerusalem, Israel.
Congregation participation	Try to get the congregation *being* the crowd. A procession obviously helps here, but it can easily be achieved without. It may need a little gentle encouragement to remove our English reserve, but it will be well worth the effort!
Focus on the contrasts	The power of the Passion narratives lies to a large extent in the reversals that take place. In a talk focus on one of the reversals below, and exploit its emotional or dramatic content: ❑ a supportive and condemning crowd ❑ Jesus as king and servant ❑ religious leaders with and without power ❑ shouting and silence ❑ Jesus in triumph and Jesus weeping
Characters at the cross	Pick out one character at the cross who may have been present in the procession. Focus on that person and his/her reaction to the events and to Jesus. This could be done in drama or with music. You could use an appropriate taped song for meditation.
A dramatic service	Why not make the whole service dramatic? The congregation becomes the crowd. Pharisees can enter trying to stop the noise. The congregation can easily imagine a donkey, so there is no need to get a real one!

PALM SUNDAY FAMILY SERVICE

The following pages outline a service held to celebrate Palm Sunday. The service enables the congregation to feel the emotions of being part of a large crowd with a celebratory feel. The congregation thus subtly becomes the crowd, which has a striking effect when the Pharisees burst in telling them to be quiet! Read the outline through, and you will pick up the feel. There is no need to follow slavishly all the ideas represented here. Use them to spark off thoughts for your own situation.

The service has three distinct parts, though these are only known to the two leaders and the music team. The service lasts about fifty minutes. It will need to be well rehearsed, and extensive use of an overhead projector (OHP) is made throughout.

Banners will help the feel of the occasion; they could depict Jesus on the donkey, which may save having a real Jesus being acted out if drama is used.

Try creating a 'feel' for the setting, with a background of Judean hills drawn on lengths of lining paper, hung around the church. The pulpit could be decorated to look like a palm tree. Have an acetate already showing, as people walk in, with a picture of the temple on it, so that it feels as though the aisle is a road down the Mount of Olives heading into Jerusalem. Perhaps some 'desert' music could be playing. All this may help to create an expectant mood before the service even starts.

Part 1
Introduction to Palm Sunday procession:

Welcome and celebrate the birthdays of anyone under twelve years. Put their names up on an OHP and sing 'Happy Birthday'. You can move all the children to the front if you like. They form a crowd celebrating someone's birthday. Explain that during the service, they will hear a story about a different sort of crowd celebrating.

Introduce the Palm Sunday procession. Use and explain OHP acetates (see note on page 9) of:

❑ view from the Mount of Olives to Jerusalem (as Jesus would have seen it)
❑ temple (Passover, bustling with lots of people)
❑ stones (huge, where God dwelt, and which the people thought would never be destroyed)
❑ Roman soldier: the people who guarded the temple were not Jews, but Romans – enemies. The Jewish people wanted someone (a king) to kick them out!

Chants:

Introduce the shouts or chants. Sporting crowds make chants. Demonstrate using the congregation ('Oggi, Oggi, Oggi, Oi Oi Oi' or similar!). The chants of the Jerusalem crowds were similar:

'Blessed is the King who comes in the name of the Lord!'
'Peace in heav'n! *(Slight pause)* Glory in the highest! Hosanna!'

Explain the chants. 'King' represents the political world, armies; 'name of the Lord' represents authority and power; 'peace' and 'glory' are proclaimed as being in heaven, yet on earth too; and 'Hosanna' expresses this by saying: 'Lord, save us'.

The two chants are chanted by different sides of the congregation. The beat of both chants is the same, and will eventually be chanted by both sides of the congregation at the same time. Each chant is five beats long. The beat is emphasized in bold.

'**Blessed** is the **King** who **comes** in the **name** of the **Lord!**'
'**Peace** in **heav'n!** *(Slight pause)* **Glory** in the **highest! Hosanna!**'

Practice of chants: Leader 1 leads the left side of the congregation: '**Blessed** is the **King** who **comes** in the **name** of the **Lord!**'

Leader 2 leads the right side of the congregation: '**Peace** in **heav'n!** *(Slight pause)* **Glory** in the **highest! Hosanna!**'

Enjoy some repartee with the congregation! The leaders ask each other, 'Did you hear anything out there?' 'I thought I heard something but it was so faint I may have been wrong,' etc. Get good chants going, then stop them, and inform the congregation that at the given point in the reading they are to shout or chant again.

The OHP acetates used to explain the background can now be used again while the reading is taking place, to give visual impact to it. The reading is adapted from Luke 19:28-44.

Reading: The disciples brought a donkey to Jesus, threw their cloaks on to it, and put Jesus on it. *(OHP – Jesus on donkey)* As Jesus went along, people spread their cloaks on the road. When he came near the place where the road goes down the Mount of Olives *(OHP)* the whole crowd of disciples began joyfully to praise God in loud voices for all the miracles they had seen, saying *(Congregation join in)*:

'Blessed is the King who comes in the name of the Lord!' and 'Peace in heav'n! Glory in the highest! Hosanna!'

The left and right sides chant alternately then together, until a good chant is going. Then actors dressed in barristers' wigs and robes (Pharisees were religious legal experts!) enter from the rear of the church.

Drama:	*Pharisee 1:*	Hoy! What do you think all this noise is about? All this shouting is disturbing the peace!
	Leader 1:	Disturbing the peace?! But we are proclaiming peace. Jesus, the Messiah King, is coming to enter Jerusalem.
	Pharisee 2:	Blasphemous nonsense. My colleagues and I are experts in religious law. Huh, lawyers! Don't you think we will know a real Messiah king when we see one? Look at this Jesus – he's nothing but a scruffy tramp on a donkey! Some Messiah King! And you're his army, are you?

Leader 1:	He is the Messiah king. Haven't you seen all the miracles he's done? No one could do such things unless they were the Messiah.
Pharisee 1:	Miracles? Trouble-making, more like! On the sabbath, weren't they? In a synagogue, weren't they? No, this is no Messiah. This is blasphemy! You insult our religion and our God! Now stop this hysteria and hooliganism now! *(All freeze)*

Reading (continued): Some of the Pharisees in the crowd said to Jesus, 'Teacher, tell your disciples to stop this!' But Jesus replied, 'I tell you, if these people keep quiet, then even the stones will cry out...'

Drama (continued):

Leader 1:	We believe this is the Messiah. Haven't you read in the prophet Zechariah: 'Rejoice greatly... shout, Daughter of Jerusalem! See, your king comes to you, righteous and bringing salvation, gentle and riding on a donkey...' This is why we rejoice and shout *(Leader 1 gets his side of congregation to join in)*: 'Blessed is the King who comes in the name of the Lord!' and
Leader 2 & rest of congregation:	'Peace in heaven! Glory in the highest! Hosanna!'
Pharisee 1:	You're wrong! Stop this blasphemy! We are your religious leaders, not this Jesus fellow! He's caused enough trouble already; don't make things worse! Come on now, break it up!
Leader 1:	You're just jealous, aren't you? This Jesus has got more authority than you have, and you don't like it, do you? Well, we believe him, and we're following him right into Jerusalem!
Pharisee 2:	We'll see how far you'll follow him, once we get to work on him.
Pharisees together:	Messiah? Never! King? What a king! *(Chants start again)* Quiet! I tell you! I tell you! Quiet! *(Chants continue)* You haven't heard the last of this!

The chants continue – alternately, then together. When a good chant is going, lead into...

Songs: Don't leave gaps between the songs. You can lead children or the whole congregation in a procession around the church if you like.

'Make Way' *(Start marching with children. Wave palms)*
'Allelu, Allelu... Praise ye the Lord'
'Hosanna!'
'You are the King of Glory' *(Sing much more slowly the second time)*
Spontaneous prayer and praise, if appropriate

Part 2

Introduction:	*Leader 1:*	We've had lots of praising and cheering for Jesus, both here in church and in the reading. We've seen how some people, the Pharisees, the religious leaders, experts in religious law, tried to stop the people praising Jesus and hailing him

Reading: (OHP – *view of Jerusalem from Mount of Olives*) As Jesus approached Jerusalem and saw the city, he wept (OHP – *weeping*) over it, and said, 'If you, even you, had only known on this day what would have brought you peace (OHP – *showing words like 'repentance', 'forgiveness', 'Jesus' – Pause*) – but now it is hidden (*Cover OHP*) from your eyes. The days will come upon you, when your enemies (OHP – *soldier*) will build an embankment against you (*Pause*) and encircle you (OHP – *invasion*) and hem you in on every side (*Pause*). They will dash you to the ground (OHP – *captives: relief from Titus' conquest – Pause*), you and the children within your walls. They will not leave one stone on another, because (*Pause – OHP of three crosses*) you did not recognize the time of God's coming to you.'

Short address (Leader 1):

Odd reaction

Don't you think that Jesus' reaction was rather odd? All these people shouting and chanting, proclaiming him King. Wouldn't he have been happy? Why cry? Well, I think Jesus knew that people didn't really want him to be the sort of king that he actually was.

Luke says that the crowds praised God for all the miracles they had seen. Well! The Pharisees didn't like that! They felt threatened. They were the religious leaders, yet people were listening to someone else – someone with power and authority. So they tried to silence him – and his followers.

The disciples did the same (Mark 9). Does Jesus tell the man to stop it? No. 'Whoever is not against us is for us.'

And us? It's easy to criticize the Pharisees. But what about us? How would we react if someone came into this church, and healed people, or even cast out demons from members of this congregation? I wouldn't mind betting that the reaction of the religious leaders and ourselves would be very similar to that portrayed in this story. We'd say: 'Stop it! Get him out! Trouble-maker!' – just like the Pharisees.

People

The people wanted this great miracle worker, this king, to come into Jerusalem and use these great powers to clear out the Romans, the political powers. But they didn't want him to change their religious situation. Jesus prophesied that exactly the opposite of what the people wanted to happen would happen. They wanted him to kick out the Romans from their religious institution. In fact, their religious power would be crushed by the very political power they wanted Jesus to remove.

Jesus wept because he knew that most people's hearts did not want to accept him for the Messiah King he really was – to bring healing, and forgiveness, and peace, and God's glory.

Human beings saw a thriving, religious centre. Jesus saw religious show, pride, arrogance, hearts that needed to repent.

Application today

Do we really want Jesus as our King? He will almost certainly not do what we expect him to do! We can't manipulate him for our own ends – either as individuals or as a church. Do we really want him to enter our lives, and our church, as King this Palm Sunday? He might need to turn the tables on us!

You know, Jesus might still be weeping. He wept because the people of Jerusalem had grabbed religion for their own ends. The temple had become their possession, not a place of genuine worship to God. And Jesus may still be weeping as he looks at his church, as people have grabbed it and used it for their own ends. And I believe Jesus may still be weeping, saying, 'Please give me my church back.' Are we prepared to do that? The first place to start is for us to give our own individual lives back to him.

Short address (Leader 2): **Crowd**

It's easy to be part of a crowd, cheering the hero. But if the hero doesn't perform as expected, crowds can easily turn their support into opposition.

Who are we like? Are we like the Pharisees, wanting to control Jesus? Or like the crowd, wanting Jesus to do what we want rather than what he wants? Will we let Jesus into our lives and our church, knowing he might change us? It's easy to wave a palm branch; it's not so easy to carry a cross.

Part 3

Prayer: Use a prayer as appropriate.

Songs: 'In my life, Lord, be glorified' *(Slowly, meditatively)*
'Jesus we enthrone you' *(First time slowly and meditatively; build up in the second verse)*

Blessing: Collection and prayer

Song: 'O Lord our God, how majestic is your name'

Meditation

As one we meet together in our worship.
As one we join together in your name.
As one we say 'Amen' to all presented.
As one we get up and go home again.

As one the people battled just to see him.
As one they called and shouted out his name.
As one they reached for palm leaves from
the tree tops.
As one they all got up and went home again.

As one the people clamoured for his torture.
As one the people shouted: 'Crucify!'
As one the people reached for stones to club
him.
As one the people stood and watched him
die.

Did those crowds simply follow one another?

Did those people really know the king they
claimed?
As they dumped their coats and lined the
road before him,
Did they do it because the others did the
same?

And are we also like-minded worshippers
today?
Thronging to the latest battle cry?
As we worship do we know the king we
claim?
Do we know the one we follow, and do we
know why?

As one let's choose to walk the path his way.
As one let's recognize the plan he holds.
As one let's dump desires to follow crowds.
As one let's serve together – and alone.

MAUNDY THURSDAY

Choral work

If the music of the church is strong enough, how about a major devotional choral work (e.g. Handel's *Messiah* or Steiner's *Crucifixion*) open to the whole community, not just the congregation? There's no need for a talk at the end – just let God speak through the music and its words.

Intimate atmosphere

If celebrating Holy Communion, try moving the furniture to create a more intimate feel. This may only be possible in the church hall, or a smaller room. Put a table in the middle of the room, with chairs for the congregation in a semi-circle (or full circle) around it. Leave one chair empty to represent Judas.

Agape meal with Communion

Share a meal together, interspersed with readings and songs. This needs to be well organized. Arrange for people to bring specific foods (e.g. savouries, salads or sweets) and ensure that there is enough to share with those who cannot provide any food of their own.

Agape meal in pub

Get away from the church into a more likely setting for the Last Supper! Using a pub allows people to invite friends to more familiar territory. You could encourage home groups to book up such a venue themselves, inviting friends. This will probably help the fellowship of such groups. There's no need for an evangelistic talk; just explain what the fellowship meal represents. The guests could be invited to church the next day to find out what happens after Maundy Thursday...

Passover meal

Many churches now celebrate a Passover style meal, possibly with Holy Communion as well. CMJ (Church's Ministry among the Jews) have a number of Messianic Jews who are able to help explain the symbolism of the Passover and its relevance to Christ. Book up early, as the demand is high at this time of year. The address is CMJ, 30c Clarence Road, St Albans, Herts AL1 4JJ.

Foot washing

To emphasize mutual service, foot washing can take place among the congregation. People may find this difficult – even offensive!

So did Peter! Perhaps this experience could be a necessary one for many of us. It may also be helpful and challenging for a congregation to see their minister or leader kneeling to wash feet.

Hand washing

If washing feet is too sensitive an issue, try hand washing. Bowls can be left at two or three points near the front, and as people come forward, they have their hands washed and dried by another member of the congregation. They in turn wash and dry the hands of the person behind them. Once their hands have been washed, they return to their place, or (if in the context of a Communion service) proceed to receive Communion. This can be a very moving experience. The 'hands' theme could be continued into Good Friday and Easter Day.

Gethsemane prayer

Try following any of the previous services with Gethsemane prayer. Leave the place where the meal or service was held, and go into a darkened room, the church garden or the church. Perhaps maintain a prayer vigil for three hours, when people are tired after the previous event(s). This enables people to identify with the disciples. The time could be spent praying particularly for those suffering in the congregation at that time.

Abrupt endings

Whatever event or service you decide on, think about finishing it abruptly. Jesus was taken away. The disciples were left in the darkness, wondering what would happen. Try to recreate the feeling. Finish the prayer vigil in silence, and depart home; end the meal or service in silence, maintained while people leave; or finish the service with drama that itself ends in an abrupt way.

Timberman

Working the wood with axe and blade
you gave life and form to dead wood.
Carving, cutting, causing the timber to yield
to your design. With steadying grip
and an eye for the grain
you called forth beauty and strength.
The craftsman at his trade.

Did you ever guess?
Did you know we would
　　beat you as wood,
　　break you as wood,
cut you and curse you.
No one to nurse you now.
Hanging.
Your carcass conformed to the grain
of hate and fear.

How we despised you, Timberman.

Miracle man.
Yielding to the pain.
Taking the weight of our evil,
and the sting from our flesh.

And as we flayed you –
the whip singing with our rage,
so your heart sang too
with the song of pain,
the song of agony,
the song of love.

The song of a man who made the wood
so that he could hang on it
for our own good.

These hands

(a meditation from Luke 22:19-21)

He took bread
and broke it.
'This is my body.'

In the same way
after supper
he took the cup.

'This cup
is the new covenant
in my blood.

But the hand of him
who is going to betray me
is with mine
upon the table.'

———————

A hand.

A hand he'd grasped
in friendship.

A hand made
for usefulness,
misused in stealing
from the common purse.

Money,
given in love,
taken in greed.
Greed that grasped
for silver,
thirty shining pieces
tight
in hand.

————

Other hands
are on this table too,
made strong
from boats and booms,
from raising sails
and hauling in the catch.
Careful hands
for mending nets;
quick hands for gutting.

Hands put to new use
for the Master;
to help the frail
and feed the hungry.

Hands
to hold the boat
steady in the wind.
Pulpit for a preacher!

Hands
newly taught to pray –
resting with his
at supper
now.

————

Peter –
what of *your* hands?

Indignant,
you refused
his washing of your feet.
Humbled,
you asked for hands and head
Christ's bathing.

You will remember that
with this night's business
done.

In sloth
your hands will be a pillow
when called to earnest prayer.

In anger
your hands will wield a sword.
Violence in Gethsemane.

In fear
your hands will wave aside
a servant girl.
Oaths of denial.

In utter shame,
head buried in these hands,
cock crowing
at tomorrow's
dawn,
tears will wash them –

your hands,
with Christ's
upon the supper table.

———————

A table.

Do I see your hands,
Master Carpenter of Nazareth,
play upon that wood,
feel the grain,
test the joints,
admiring finish and design?

Here are hands
strong from the
bench,
from saw and plane,
chisel, mallet;
artists
in wood.

These hands
held a child in blessing;
gave back
to grieving parents
a daughter
from the dead;
caressed unseeing eyes
in gentle love
'till Bartimaeus saw again.

These hands
touched lepers;
traced figures in the sand
while the adulterer's accusers
slunk sullenly from sight;
broke five small loaves
and made a feast
five thousand places
set!

———

These hands,
Christ's hands,
his hands:
break bread,
pour wine;
reach up in anguished prayer
to take the Cup
which is his Father's will.

And in the flickering light
do these hands
hold Judas
in a final grasp of love
before the fatal
kiss?

Look at these hands
still quick to heal –

red raw
rough wrapped
by rope.
'Security,'
they say.
The Prince of Peace
secure!

———

Secure
upon a cross.

No playing now
upon this wood
no feeling of the grain
in silent admiration –

but searing
agony.

This is the work
you came to do
Lord Christ –
through wood
and nails.
Hands
held wide
in love.

———

Jesus
my hands
need washing.

Praying hands?
too often idle.

Generous hands?
too often grasping.

Useful hands?
busy with the world's
work
not yours.

Take my hands
into the hands still scarred
by nails
I drove
at Calvary,

and teach them,
like yours,
to love.

A PASSOVER MEAL

Introduction

The following texts can be used during a meal, as an event in its own right, or as a preface to Holy Communion.

A Passover meal is valuable in helping people to understand the link between Passover and Holy Communion, and the truths which lie behind the rituals and ceremonies of the two events.

Opening prayer

Lord God our Father, we meet as members of your family to share together this special meal. We are to eat the Passover in readiness for your great act of redemption, as Israel ate the night of the exodus.

We are to celebrate the Passover as Jesus did with his disciples the night in which his Passion began, his great act of salvation.

We thank you for this time of remembering, with sincere gladness and great sadness, awed by your power and humility and love.

Explanation

Introductory blessings and grace before the meal.

President: Blessed are you, Lord, God of all creation,
Maker of the fruits of the earth.
Blessed are you, Lord, God of all creation,
You have chosen us because you love us.
You have given us this food to share with you
the great festival of Passover;
the meal you shared with your closest disciples in the Upper Room,
the meal you share with us now.
Bless us, O Lord, and bless this food we are to eat.

(Candles are lit)

Assistant: As at the Passover, will all mothers stretch their hands towards the candle and ask a blessing on us.

All mothers: May the Lord be gracious and bless us.
May he make his face to shine upon us.
May he keep this his family in peace and love
for ever and ever. Amen.

The traditional question

Assistant:	A child now asks the traditional question.
First child stands to ask:	Why is this night different from all other nights?
President:	We were slaves to Pharaoh in Egypt; the Lord our God brought us out therefrom with a mighty hand and an outstretched arm. Blessed be he who keeps his promise to Israel. Blessed be he. The Holy One planned the end of bondage to fulfil the promise made to Abraham our father – 'Know of a surety that thou shall be a stranger in a land that is not theirs and shall serve them; and they shall afflict them 400 years; and also that nation, whom they shall serve will I judge; and afterwards they shall come out with great substance.'
	And also on this night Christ Jesus, our Lord, the promised Messiah, instituted the blessed sacrament of his body and blood and offered himself in sacrifice to God for our redemption, opening the gates of heaven to all mankind. Blessed be he who keeps his promise to his people Israel.
	And it is this promise which has stood by our ancestors and by us, for it was not just one person but many who rose up against us to destroy us. But the Holy One, blessed be he, delivered us from their hands.
Assistant:	And we cried unto the Lord, the God of our fathers, and the Lord heard our voice and saw our affliction and our toil, and our oppression. And the Lord brought us forth, out of the land of Egypt, with a mighty hand and with an outstretched arm, and with great terribleness, and with signs and with wonders.
President:	For how many are the increasing kindnesses bestowed upon us by the Almighty?
	If he had brought us out of Egypt and not performed great wonders...
All (respond after each phrase):	We would have thought it sufficient.
President:	If he had performed great wonders and not passed over our firstborn...
	If he had passed over our firstborn and not divided the sea for us...
	If he had divided the sea for us and not caused us to pass through it on dry land...
	If he had caused us to pass through it on dry land and not supplied our needs in the wilderness for forty years...
	If he had supplied our needs in the wilderness for forty years and not fed us with manna...
	If he had fed us with manna and not given us the sabbath to rest...
	(The remaining phrases are spoken by an Assistant with the congregation responding: 'We would have thought it sufficient.')

Assistant:	If he had given us the sabbath and not given us the Commandments... If he had given us the Commandments and not brought us into the land of Israel... If he had brought us into the land of Israel and not built the temple for us... If he had built the temple for us and not sent the Messiah to save us... If he had sent the Messiah and he had not been God's own Son... If he had sent his own Son and he had not suffered as a man for us... If he had suffered for us and not died for us... If he had died for us and not risen from the dead... If he had risen from the dead, giving us a pledge of our resurrection, and had not left us the gift of his abiding presence in the Holy Spirit and in the Eucharist...
All:	We would have thought it sufficient.
President:	How much greater is our praise and thanksgiving to the Lord, our God, for all the blessings he has heaped upon us.

The four questions

Second child stands to ask:	Why do we eat lamb on this night? What does it mean?
President:	It is to remind us that when God slew the first-born Egyptians he commanded our forefathers to roast a lamb, and eat it and to sprinkle their doorposts with its blood so that these houses were 'passed over' by God, and their firstborn were not slain. The lamb was an offering made to God when God led our forefathers out of the land of slavery. When Jesus Christ, the promised Messiah, came on earth, he offered himself as the Paschal Lamb to redeem us from sin. 'Behold the Lamb of God,' says St John. 'Behold him who takes away the sin of the world.'
Third child stands to ask:	Why do we eat Matzah, unleavened bread, on this night?
President:	We remember this flight of our forefathers from Egypt when there was no time for the dough to become leavened. It was this unleavened bread which our Lord took and blessed at the celebration of the Passover on the night before he died.
Fourth child stands to ask:	Why do we drink wine on this night? What does it mean?
President:	Wine was drunk by our forefathers to celebrate their delivery from Egypt, and it was this wine that our Lord took and blessed, and gave to his disciples.
Fifth child stands to ask:	Why do we eat bitter herbs? What do they mean?

President: When our forefathers were slaves in Egypt, their masters embittered their lives with hard labour and cruelty and oppression. We remember too the sufferings of all oppressed people in the world, especially the cruel history of the oppression of the Jewish and coloured races. We beg forgiveness for our part in this, remembering our unity with all mankind as children of God.

We dip our bitter herbs in salt water to recall the shedding of tears that suffering entails, echoing the prophecy of the Messiah as 'a man of sorrows, acquainted with grief'. We recall too the saying of Jesus, 'If any man will come after me, he must deny himself and take up his cross daily and follow me.'

The eternal message

President: In every generation it is the duty of each individual to regard himself as though he had gone forth out of Egypt as it is said, 'And thou shalt tell thy son in that day saying it is because of that which the Lord did unto me when I came forth out of Egypt.'

Assistant: For not only our ancestors did the Holy One redeem, but also did he redeem us with them, as it is said, 'And he brought us out from thence, that he might bring us in, to give the land which he swore unto our forefathers.'

President: So, brothers and sisters, with Christ Jesus and his disciples, eat this Passover supper, as men and women who have been freed from slavery, about to journey to the Promised Land, and give thanks to the Lord our God, for his mercy endures for ever.

All: Praise the Lord for he has made us free, and his mercy endures for ever.

(Source of text unknown)

GOOD FRIDAY

Continuation of the theme

Try to make Good Friday link in with a theme used over the whole week. If 'Characters at the cross' is used, posters of all the characters involved could be pinned up around the church. The congregation could process around each character, with a short meditation and/or song at each. These could be led by different members of the congregation. A similar approach could be adopted for 'Jerusalem journey' (see page 8) or any other theme.

Ecumenical march of witness

Good Friday is often used for ecumenical marches of witness. Graham Kendrick's 'Make Way for the Cross' is especially suited to Holy Week, and is both moving and powerful. Try incorporating other churches on the route, stopping off at each to concentrate on one particular aspect of the Passion, rather like the Stations of the Cross. A reading, hymn or song, and prayer at each church could be appropriate, and would enable a larger musical accompaniment than on the march itself. Calling in at various churches also enables those who cannot undertake a long procession to take a greater part. Approximate timings must of course be worked out in advance.

Stations of the Cross

All the events of Good Friday – from Pilate's judgement through to the removal of Jesus' body – provide good opportunities for reflection, prayer and teaching. Avoid sentimentality. A modified sequence of the traditional format is:

- ❑ Judgement of Pilate (Luke 23:23-25; John 19:1-16)
- ❑ Carrying the cross (John 19:17)
- ❑ Simon carrying the cross (Luke 23:26)
- ❑ Women crying (Luke 23:27-29)
- ❑ Crucifixion (Luke 23:35-43; John 19:25-27)
- ❑ Taking of Jesus' clothes (John 19:23)
- ❑ Taking of Jesus' body (Luke 23:50-54)
- ❑ Burial (Matthew 27:62-66; Luke 23:55-56)

After each section the following response can be used:

Leader: We adore you, O Christ, and praise you.
People: Because by your holy cross you have redeemed the world.

Evening service

Try an evening service of silence. The occasional meditation could be included if people find complete silence too hard. The Good Friday litany below is a pertinent reminder of our own sins, as we remember the negative attitudes of some of those involved in the events of the Passion.

Responses to litany:

Leader: O Lamb of God, who takes away the sins of the world...

Congregation: Have mercy on us.

Leader: Let us remember how the sins of many brought our Saviour to his cross, and let us ask God to reveal to us the sins in our own lives, and in the life of the church, through which our Lord is crucified again.

We remember the sin of Caiaphas and those for whom he spoke when he said, 'It is expedient for us that one man should die for the people.' Let us ask God's forgiveness for the times we have taken the easy way out, at whatever the cost to others.
O Lamb of God...

We remember the Pharisees who, in keeping the traditions of men, shared in the crucifixion of Christ. Let us ask God's forgiveness for frustrating his will for his church by clinging to our human traditions.
O Lamb of God...

We remember the sin of Judas, who betrayed his Lord with a kiss. Let us ask God's forgiveness for every way in which those who own the name of Christ have shared in his betrayal, by lip service not borne out in actions.
O Lamb of God...

We remember the sin of Peter, who denied Jesus in front of others. Let us ask God's forgiveness for our own denials, by thought, word and action, and in what we have failed to do or say through weakness and cowardice.
O Lamb of God...

We remember the sin of Pilate, who asked, 'What is truth?', while looking upon him who is the Way, the Truth, and the Life. We ask God's forgiveness for our blindness to the presence of our Lord, and the truth of his word.
O Lamb of God...

Finally, we remember the sin of the crowd who chose Barabbas before Jesus. Let us ask God's forgiveness for following the crowd, and for choosing the way of violence rather than the way of love and self-sacrifice.
O Lamb of God...

Create in us a clean heart, O God, and renew a right spirit within us. Amen.

Characters at the cross

Offer a series of short talks based on each character (possibly using drama sketches). Different members of the congregation could present each character. Perhaps spread them through the service, bracketed by songs, readings, prayers or meditations. Alternatively have an extended treatment of one single character.

Family service talk: Responses to the cross

Visual aids:	*Large cross of wood or overhead projector slides on which can be added the responses as the talk progresses*

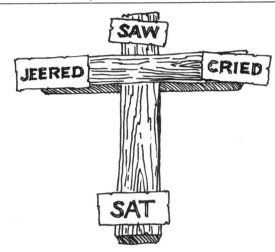

Matthew 27: 32-44

This talk links with one for Easter day using the same visual aid.

☐ Some **SAT** (Matthew 27:36). Place OHP or card at the foot of the cross. They were indifferent and unaware. It was all in a day's job – had no significance for them. It's the same today.
☐ Some **JEERED** (Matthew 27:29; Mark 15:31; Luke 23:35). Place on an arm of the cross. It's the same today.
☐ Some **CRIED** (Luke 23:27-28,48). Place on the other arm of the cross. It's the same today.
☐ Some **SAW** (Mark 15:38; Luke 23:40-42). Place at the top of the cross. Some understood something of who Jesus was and what was happening. It's the same today.

Conclusion: We fit somewhere on there, too. Where?

Family service talk: The cross-shaped hole

The set is built across the chancel and represents the inner sanctuary of the temple – the Holy of Holies. It consists of a wooden structure and black drapes approximately 3m high (see illustration). Removable blocks forming a cross are built into the central wall. The blocks will be removed during the drama to represent the tearing of the temple curtain and access for everyone into God's presence.

Introduction: Read verses from Leviticus 16 or Hebrews 9:11-14; 10:11-14 to illustrate the Old Testament rituals. Only the high priest could enter the Holy of Holies, and only once a year, to enter the place of God's special presence.

Main Talk: The thrust of the talk shows how the barrier that exists between us and God is opened up by Jesus. Thoughts, words and deeds create this barrier. As each area is discussed, a block is removed from the 'barrier' (wall), and turned around revealing that word on the back (see illustration). Each block is then placed in front of the wall, to one side. The blocks are built up to form a freestanding cross (which remains standing for the duration of the service). The final block to be removed should be the crossbeam, with the words 'It is finished' being revealed – representing forgiveness for thoughts, words and deeds. At this point a member of the congregation or an actor can walk through the cross-shaped hole into the holiest place. The way that was closed, but now open through Christ, is thus visibly demonstrated.

SIMON THE CROSSBEARER

This drama could fit with 'Characters at the cross'. Leave the congregation 'hanging' in suspense if the end of the drama is left till Easter Day. The narrator is Simon of Cyrene, as an old man. He stands in a place where he can be clearly seen (in a pulpit or on a raised area).

Beloved (children) I am going to tell you a story: a story of when I was a young man. But I remember it as clearly as if it happened yesterday. Listen carefully and perhaps you will see it, too.

My name is Simon. I come from the town of Cyrene in North Africa. One day, many years ago, I travelled from my home there, to the great city of Jerusalem. This is the capital of Israel, where the Jews had a great temple, where they worshipped God. Just as you come to church on Sundays.

I was very tired as I came through the city gate and into the crowded streets. It was very busy in the city, as crowds of Jews had collected there for a special service and meal together, called the Passover.

As I pushed my way along the roads, I noticed a distant shouting and screaming, as if men's voices were raised in anger, and women were weeping.

The noise drew nearer and nearer until I saw, from the swaying of the people in front of me, that something, or someone, was coming down the street towards me. I heard the fierce commands of Roman soldiers, shouting to people to get out of the way. *(Begin hearing Roman soldiers – out of sight – giving sharp commands)* When you heard a Roman shout like that, you did as you were told!

All the people around me rushed to get out of the way, scattering and pushing, until we were all standing along the edge of the street, peering up the road to see who was coming.

Then we caught a sight of him. *(Pause. An actor representing Jesus appears. He needs to make the journey during the following narration, around the church towards the central table or worship area, and then out of an exit door by the time the crucifixion begins)*

It was a criminal, perhaps a robber or a murderer, who was taking his last walk on earth. He was on his way to his death. He was going to be crucified.

Crucifixion is a horrible way to die. They nail or tie you on a wooden cross or a tree, and you hang there until you are too weak to breathe, and then you suffocate in agony.

Most people feel sorry for a crucified man, and we felt pity for the man who came stumbling down the road towards us. No matter what crime he had done, we wished him a quicker death.

Then I noticed something else. *(Women already in place at the ends of pews step out and join the procession. They can be in ordinary clothes. This gives both a startling, unexpected movement and emphasizes our involvement today in Jesus's death)*

Moving along the edge of the crowd, apparently following the criminal, was a group of women, weeping and calling out to the man.

It was then that I heard what they were saying. 'Jesus, Master, Jesus, Jesus,' they were weeping.

Now I had heard of Jesus. Stories were told of how he had made the blind see; the deaf hear; even the lame walk. A man from God, so it was said. What was he doing here? Why was he on his way to a criminal's death? What had he done that was wrong? *(An actor miming the part of Simon half rises from his seat)*

I watched him... *(Jesus falls where Simon-mimer is standing)* He fell... He tried to rise... He could not get up because he was so weak from the cruel whipping the soldiers had given him.

He looked a horrible sight. Blood dripped down his face, from a circle of thorns, twisted round his forehead. His back was a mass of open wounds. He grimaced with pain... and I found... I couldn't take my eyes from his face... *(Roman guard comes towards Simon and grabs him roughly)*

I did not see the Roman soldier coming towards me. A hand roughly grabbed my arm and I was hauled out of the crowd. I dared not protest. If I tried to resist, I would have felt the whiplash on my back. I was ordered to lift the fallen cross. *(Guard fiercely shouts the command to pick it up)*

I bent to raise it and struggled to lay it across my shoulders.

I did not dare to help the man, who lay underneath it. But he looked up, straight into my eyes, and I saw that he was grateful, that I should carry the heavy burden of his cross.

Brothers and sisters, I have never forgotten that moment. I would bear his cross again today, and every day, to help him. *(Mimers move slowly up the aisle)*

We struggled together, on down the street, out of the city, and up the hill to Golgotha. And all the while, the soldiers swore at us, the crowd watched, the women wept and the political Jewish leaders, who had plotted his death, jeered to see him brought to such degradation. *(If there are enough people to take part, they can be seated in the congregation and stand to shake their fist, then sit again)*

My heart burned within me... Why?

Why should God allow this good man to die? The stories one heard of him were always of his love and goodness. Why was an innocent man to suffer, when wicked men went unpunished?

(Mimers should have processed around the circuit of the church and reached an exit, so that mimers are out of sight for the sound effects of crucifixion. This can be taped and put out on the church PA system or be done from the vestry)

Hands

I cried out.
My screams filled the air.
Oh, not aloud,
Not audible anguish, you understand.
No.
Silent screams
From one heart to another.
I needed a hand,
A hand that cared
From outside of me... and my small world.

And in an instant
He was there.
Reaching out his hand.
Just the hand I'd been waiting for.
Perhaps it had always been there.
Perhaps I had just not seen it before.
Had not had the eyes for it.

And in response
I reached up.
My hand to his.
My pleading, empty, desperate fingers,
Screaming for a touch...

Oh!
His hand surprised mine.
His hand was different.
This hand was broken. Bruised.
Calloused from a workman's bench.
Ingrained with sweat and sawdust.
And worse.

Blood.
This hand was stained.
Red.
Scarred and scratched.

Battered from the hammer's blow.
A carpenter's hammer...
Or was it a soldier's?
And there were cracks.
And a hole.
The marks of love and hate.

They had seen life,
These fingers.
Life and death.
Had touched the face of sinners;
Held the sores of lepers;
And stroked the skin of sad and sinful men.

My fingers hadn't.
They recoiled at such things.
Despite myself I drew back.
I had thought he was my friend.
On my side.
But our hands told a different story.

Mine were washed, supple,
Cleanly superficial.
White with self-concern.
His were dirty.
From loving.

To touch those hands
Might contaminate.
Would contaminate.
It would affect my fingers.
And my heart too.
And my hands, once held by his,
Might be treated like his.
Scoffed at; soiled and scorned.
Broken – until they too were able
To bear those marks – the marks of love.

EASTER: INTRODUCTION

Introduction

Easter Saturday is so often relegated to being simply the day in between. Good Friday completes Holy Week and Easter Sunday is the next important event. Try, however, to make Easter Saturday special. It will be a busy day for shopping and preparation so plan well in advance. Make the decorating of the church something different. A service of preparation on Easter Saturday evening can be a most rewarding experience. There may well be time during the day for some outreach.

Easter Sunday is, of course, the day! A sunrise service, a meeting at a riverside, baptisms, and breakfast can all make the beginning of the day special. Most churches have an Easter Sunday family service.

A lot of effort is put into this so that there is little time and energy left for the rest of the day. The evening of the day of resurrection stands out in the Bible. Make every effort to make this important in your own fellowship. Three suggestions – a dramatic reading, a meditation, and an Easter carol service – are included.

Easter Monday is becoming more and more associated with congested roads and expensive entertainment. Try to make it a family day for the church fellowship. Parties don't have to be kept for Christmas and birthdays.

Easter week means no school or playgroups. This is an ideal opportunity for an Easter adventure week with the children and young people. Run it from Tuesday to Friday. The Sunday after Easter is often called Low Sunday. Make it special by involving all those who have joined in the Easter adventure week.

Death and resurrection – an allegory

There was a small community which lived together simply and fairly happily at the beginning of a valley. Just beyond this settlement the valley led up to a huge and mysterious range of mountains. They were always covered in cloud and conveyed a sense of the mysterious and the unknown.

Access to the mountains was prevented by precipitous cliffs on either side. Between them across the valley was an insurmountable wall. But in the wall was a DOOR.

Regularly the elderly went to that DOOR and passed through. Sometimes younger people went, even babies. Some went willingly, some very unwillingly. Whoever went through never came back.

The DOOR was a place of fear and loss. It was the gateway to a fearful unknown. As such it was rarely talked about or, if it was, it was given a less stark name than the DOOR.

It was rumoured that some in the settlement had darkened rooms and were doing all manner of eerie things, like making contact with some of those who had gone through, but the contacts seemed trivial and unsatisfying.

Some people said there was nothing beyond it; others said there was nothing to be concerned about; and others that it was 'best not to speak about it'.

One day someone was born into the community who was somehow different, different in who he was, what he said and did. He was loving and compassionate. He had amazing insights into situations and people. He did extraordinary things; a very unusual human being.

He said that anyone who believed in what he stood for need not be afraid of the DOOR. He, and he alone, could safely see them through it. He claimed there was something beyond which could be incredibly wonderful or just the opposite.

He didn't stop there. He became too outspoken, too uncomfortable to have around. Those in charge began to get uncomfortable, too. After much scheming they dragged him off to the DOOR and tossed him through it. That would be the end of him. No one ever came back!

Some of his companions went near the DOOR a few days later and said they had seen him. Recognizable but different. He had come back through the DOOR alive! He had broken its power!

Most did not believe it. He clearly wasn't around as before. His friends were sure he was alive. And then when it was their turn to go through the DOOR, he was seen going through it with them.

It made all the difference. Their life in the community was no longer dominated by fear of the DOOR, they actually looked forward to going through it. It was as if a great enemy had been defeated.

Banners for Easter

Banners for your church will not only be something of beauty and a witness, but will also be a means of special growth and development for those who spent time in their preparation. Encourage this but allow adequate time. The designs can also be used for illustrations in your church magazine, service sheets and Easter publicity. The Easter Monday allegory 'Death and resurrection' can be depicted with the help of banners (see previous page).

Start with the Bible and with prayer. Read the events surrounding Easter and pray for inspiration. Make a note of your thoughts and ideas. You are wanting to declare Good News; this is important to you. Your images are to proclaim Jesus. Make sure that each word will explain itself.

Making your banner is not the same as sewing a pretty picture, collage or wall-hanging, but is an important part of mission. The design must be simple and uncluttered and speak of new life; of joy; of light. It should make the Easter message worth enquiring about and worth remembering.

The size you choose will depend on your church. It needs to be clearly visible. Rectangular banners hang best. For the letters, pin on templates before you commit yourself. Cutting the material then needs to be accurate. It is best to keep lettering in one colour, though contrasting edging can make them stand out. Above all, make them legible.

Experiment until you get the effect you want and then give yourself plenty of time to make up the banner. Finish it off neatly and line it to make it hang better. Enjoy your work, and your banner will reflect this joy.

Consider the colours of the season and of your church. Background colours and fabric are important (see 'Guide to Colours' on this page). Purple is the traditional colour for Lent; white and gold are the Easter colours. Pure white as a background is rather stark, so a shade off will be better. Green or yellow/gold can be effective. Be careful with the dark colours and shiny materials.

Any bright spring colours can be used for the design. Try to make the banner sparkle. Gold cords and braids shine; sequins catch the light; some fabrics have a sheen. These will give greater impact.

Some of the motifs used have a symbolic meaning. Ivy is a symbol of eternal life because of its continual green colour; the dandelion reminds us of bitter herbs, a symbol of the Passion; the bright yellow flower speaks of the resurrection coming from the Passion; the vine and the grapes represent the blood of Christ; the wheat reminds us of bread representing the body of Christ; the fish is an early Christian symbol.

The banners illustrated on page 33 are only ideas! They can be adapted in many ways to suit your needs.

Note: Line drawings from the Good News Bible may be used if prior permission is obtained from the Bible Society, Stonehill Green, Westlea, Swindon SN5 7BR. The books on banner-making (see page 48) by Priscilla Nunnerly are a good source of ideas and information.

GUIDE TO COLOURS

Black
solemnity, mourning, sin, death

White
humility, purity, holiness, innocence, peace, mercy, rejoicing

Blue
heavenly love, heaven, divinity and grace

Brown
renunciation of the world, spiritual death, autumn, the past

Gold
kingship, majesty, glory, heaven, divine righteousness

Grey
ashes, humility, mourning

Green
spring, life, regeneration, hope

Purple
royalty, imperial power, passion, suffering

Red
love, hate, sovereign power, danger, combat, suffering, fire

Yellow
promise, celebration, light

EASTER SATURDAY

Decorations

Saturday is the day when the church gets decorated for Sunday, and usually there is an abundance of spring flowers. Many churches are keen on flower festivals and so encourage a theme in the floral decorations. Many people are very artistic and have wonderful ways of portraying abstract ideas or, on the other hand, illustrating incidents and events. If there has been a holiday club for children during Holy Week encourage the incorporation of their activity work in your Easter decoration.

Try the following:

❑ **the resurrection appearances:** the tomb in the garden; the upper room; the road to Emmaus; the seashore

❑ **four important days:** Maundy Thursday (bread/wine/meal); Good Friday (wood/cross/nails); Easter Saturday (darkness/mourning); Easter Sunday (resurrection/light/glory)

❑ **the themes of the vigil:** creation; fall; judgement; sacrifice; covenant

❑ **events in Holy Week:** the triumphal entry; cleansing of the temple; foot washing; Last Supper; crucifixion; resurrection

❑ **gardens:** the garden of creation (God made everything good); the garden of conflict (Gethsemane – the arrest of Jesus); the garden of conquest (resurrection garden/life) or the garden of Eden (creation); the garden of evil (Gethsemane); the garden of Easter (resurrection)

❑ **themes which are linked to the Passion and resurrection:** lamb of God (John 1:29); shepherd (John 10:11); corn of wheat (John 12:24); bread of life (John 6:35; Mark 14:22); vine (John 15); the resurrection and the life (John 11:25-26)

This kind of 'mini' flower festival could encourage people to stay behind after the Sunday morning service. Take the opportunity to explain the floral arrangements. The church could also be open on Easter Sunday afternoon and during the week.

Cracking the egg

If the real meaning of Christmas is not understood by many people today, then Easter is even more of a mystery to them. Encourage a group from your church to try a simple street research on Easter Saturday during peak shopping time, or encourage them to go to a local park or stand outside a pub and catch people that way. Brief them carefully.

- Ask one simple straightforward question: 'What does Easter mean to you?'
- Accept whatever answer is offered without further question.
- Be ready for people to brush you to one side.
- Offer an attractive leaflet explaining Easter.
- Don't give these away except as the follow-up to your question.
- Don't enter into discussion and argument.

Useful and attractive leaflets can be obtained from the Christian Publicity Organization, Garcia Estate, Canterbury Road, Worthing, West Sussex BN13 1BW. The Bible Society also produces attractive leaflets and the *Challenge* newspaper (Easter edition) can be a useful giveaway (available from Challenge Literature Fellowship, Revenue Buildings, Chapel Road, Worthing, West Sussex BN11 1BQ).

Saturday evening

This can be a very special time. More and more churches are finding an Easter vigil and the service of Light a helpful way of linking Good Friday and Holy Week to Easter Day. Details can be found in *Lent, Holy Week and Easter* (SPCK).

A less formal service may be appropriate. Try a quiet, meditative preparation linking Good Friday to Easter Sunday. Use the three objects below with appropriate comment and allow time for quiet reflection:

- **towel** – Jesus washing the disciples' feet, making himself a servant, humble and vulnerable
- **bread** – the Last Supper, broken bread, Christ's body broken and given for us
- **nail** – his physical sufferings for us, his even greater suffering in his separation from God because of our sin.

In the quietness allow the lights to be dimmed. After a suitable time the minister goes in silence to the main entrance. The Easter candle is lit with the words:

'May the light of Christ, rising in glory, banish all darkness from our hearts and minds.'

The candle is brought slowly up to the front of the church. If it seems helpful, a suitable song can be sung or Psalm 27 read together. People are encouraged to leave quietly, but with a sense of thanksgiving and quiet rejoicing in their hearts.

EASTER SUNDAY

A surprise package

Build up anticipation and excitement by producing the biggest box you can manage. At an appropriate time in the family service open it to release a mass of helium-filled balloons. On their tails are cards inscribed with 'Alleluia' on both sides. The balloons will fly skywards and stay up in the roof of your building for weeks.

Interviews

Try interviewing some New Testament characters who witnessed the death and burial of Jesus, followed by some of the disciples who saw him alive. Complete it by interviewing one or, at the most, two people who know him to be alive today. Get the interviewer to be as realistic as possible, playing the part of someone out on the street trying to get material for a TV/radio programme or a newspaper.

Select what you have time for from the following:

Pilate: 'The crowd wanted Barabbas and so I had to let Jesus die.'
Centurion: 'He was dead all right – I killed him.'
Joseph of Arimathea: 'He was buried in my own tomb and I saw that the stone was in place.'
Roman officer: 'I set the guard and they wouldn't dare let anyone near.'
Mary: 'I saw the stone rolled away.'
John: 'I saw the empty tomb.'
Peter: 'I saw the grave clothes and the body gone.'
Mary: 'I spoke to the angels.'
Thomas: 'I saw the nail prints in his hands.'
Cleopas: 'He had a meal with us.'
Today's witness: 'He has made all the difference to my life.'

Investigation

Have two people dressed up: one as Sherlock Holmes, complete with deerstalker, pipe, glass and scarf, and the other dressed as a bloodhound (suitable gear could be hired from a fancy dress shop). The bloodhound's name is Watson. The dog leads Holmes to five clues set around the church building and, as each is discovered, is rewarded with a small chocolate egg.

The clues can either be quite small and built up into a display at the front of church as they are discovered, or they can be life-size and various members of the congregation can be used. But they will need to be primed well in advance and rehearsed.

- **The stone.** If this is a full-size replica, then there will need to be some acting as this is moved with difficulty, though it may be made of cardboard! Explain that it was impossible to move it without help as it would have been sealed and, in any case, it would have had to be rolled uphill. So it was impossible for Jesus to have got out of the grave on his own.
- **Soldiers.** Could they have been bribed? Clearly, their lives were at stake. They would have let the body go neither to the enemies of Jesus or his friends.
- **The grave clothes.** They were still there and showed clearly that they were undisturbed either by someone stealing the body or by Jesus struggling to get out.
- **The disciples who saw Jesus alive.** Peter, John, Mary, Thomas, Cleopas and his friend, the other disciples and even 500 at one time all saw Jesus. They saw his familiar identifying features, they heard him speak and they ate with him.
- **The Christian church today.** Many members in the service are witnesses to that. If possible, have one member give a short testimony.

The clues can be built up to eliminate the impossible and to help people understand that only one conclusion can be drawn: Jesus is alive. Add that Jesus said he would come back to life. This proves that he is God's Son, that he is alive today, and that he died to give us life.

Acrostic on Easter

This is based on John 20:1-20. Build the words up one by one and help people to discover the hidden word. Make sure your letters are large enough for those at the back of church to see. Always use lowercase lettering.

Mary discovered the Empty tomb
Mary saw the Angels
Mary heard the Saviour
Mary Told the others
Jesus Entered the room
The disciples Recognized him

Believing the impossible

Get the congregation to imagine trying to sell a bicycle to a group of people who have never seen one before. People would have lots of reasons for not buying it, such as:

- It can't stand up by itself.
- It's a complicated piece of equipment.
- People will laugh at me if I try to ride it.
- What's the use of it anyway?

Involve as many people as possible and get plenty of suggestions. You may feel you want to brief in advance one or two people to help you. Conclude this part of the talk by getting someone to ride the bicycle.

Show that the resurrection is like the bicycle. That, too, is unlikely – people will laugh at me if I believe it – what's the use of it? – no one ever came back from the dead before. Lead on to explain that only when we believe it and experience Christ alive does the resurrection make real sense.

Eggs – twice laid!

Start by talking about Easter eggs: who has got some; who has eaten any, etc.

Show an egg box full of eggs. Only one is hard boiled.

What comes out of an egg? Did you know that a chicken has to be born twice?

Select one of the eggs (preferably the hard-boiled one!). Throw it in the air a few times, and catch it carefully, to create the illusion that it is fragile!

All chickens have to be born twice. Once when the egg comes out of its mum, and then again when the chick comes out of its shell. Imagine being inside the egg – it feels cozy and warm, it's a nice, familiar place, a place to call your own – it's comfortable.

The chick could happily go on living inside the egg for ever. It has been born once and life isn't too bad in the egg. But the chick will only really come alive when it gets born a second time. It needs to break out of its shell. If it stays in there it will never be really alive. If a chick inside the egg says, 'I think I will stay here for ever,' it will completely miss the point of being born in the first place.

People are the same. Most people are like the chick inside the egg. They feel life is OK, warm, comfortable, secure, not bad. But Jesus said that people need to be born again. When a person is born again it is like a chick coming out of its shell. Life really begins. Being born again means coming alive to God, and finding for the first time the life God wants you to live and enjoy.

End by throwing an apparently unboiled egg at a member of the congregation, or smashing an unboiled egg on the head of a church dignitary!

Special eggs

Use three cardboard Easter eggs which are of a reasonable size.

In the first one place a piece of bread and talk about the Last Supper.

In the second put a small cross and speak about Christ's death on the cross.

The third Easter egg is empty. Talk about the empty tomb.

Expect the unexpected

This talk highlights what Mary expected and what she found on that first Easter day. Develop the four contrasting couplets below. Print the words 'expected/found' clearly on card. Each pair should be written with 'expected' above 'found'. First reveal the expected phrase, then unfold the card to reveal the found phrase underneath, as you tell of Mary's surprises one by one.

She **expected** to find the grave closed and sealed.
She **found** it open, the stone rolled away.

She **expected** to find the body wrapped up on the ledge.
She **found** the clothes there but no body.

She **expected** to be alone.
But she **found** someone else there, too.

She **expected** to find Jesus dead.
She **found** him alive.

God surprised Mary and turned her life upside-down. He changed her tears to laughter, and fear to joy. She knew Jesus was alive and life was never the same again.

What were you expecting this Easter? What have you found?

Family service talk: Alive, well and true

Visual aids:	*Large cross of wood or overhead projector slides on which can be added the responses as the talk progresses*

Matthew 28:1-10

This story follows on from the Good Friday talk: Responses to the cross (page 26). It can also be used on its own. If used with the Good Friday talk, remind the congregation of the words placed on the cross then.

- ❑ **Alive** (Matthew 28:6; Luke 24:5). Place the OHP or card on an arm of the cross. Recount the story. Note the certainty of some of the disciples that Jesus was alive. How amazing!
- ❑ **Well** (John 20:27). Place on the other arm of the cross. Note that he was not a half-dead person. How amazing!
- ❑ **True** (John 20:29; 1 Corinthians 15:3-4,17). Place at the top of the cross. How amazing!

Conclusion: This was a unique event. How amazing!

CAIAPHAS' CATASTROPHIC CAPER

Cast: Delilah and Benjamin – two teenagers; Caiaphas – a chief priest.
Delilah is standing waiting. Enter Benjamin running.

Benjamin:	Delilah, Delilah, Delilah, Delilah. *(Collides with Delilah knocking her over)*
Delilah:	Benjamin! Why don't you watch where you're going?
Benjamin:	Oh, don't worry about that. I've got some great news.
Delilah:	Don't tell me, Bethlehem won last night.
Benjamin:	No! More important than camel racing!
Delilah:	Well, I never thought I'd hear you say anything was more important than camel racing.
Benjamin:	Will you just shut up and listen. I've seen him! He's alive!
Delilah:	Seen who?
Benjamin:	Jesus. He's alive!
Delilah:	I don't believe you.
Benjamin:	But why, why, why, Delilah?
Delilah:	Because, because, because Benjamin, Jesus is dead, remember? He was killed last week.
Benjamin:	I know that, but now he's alive.
Delilah:	Benjamin, how can he be alive? Is this some sort of joke? Because if it is, I don't think it's funny.
Benjamin:	Of course it's not a joke. *(Enter Caiaphas who stands at a distance listening)* Look, I was at a meeting with Peter and loads of Jesus' friends, when suddenly he was in the room with us. And he wasn't a ghost because he ate some fish, and even Thomas believed it, so there!
Caiaphas:	Hello, young man. I couldn't help overhearing you just now. Did you say you'd seen Jesus?
Benjamin:	Yes. I was in this room with... *(Delilah clasps her hand over Benjamin's mouth and pulls him away)* What are you doing?
Delilah:	Do you know who that is? That is Caiaphas, one of the people who had Jesus killed. He works at the temple.
Benjamin:	Are you sure?

Delilah:	Yes! Don't tell him anything.
Caiaphas:	Well, young man, have you seen Jesus? Have you? Have you?
Benjamin:	Why do you want to know? So you can kill all his friends like you killed him? Only it didn't work because he's alive again!
Caiaphas:	Ah, so you admit it, eh? I think it's time you came with me.
Benjamin:	No, never.

There is a struggle. Caiaphas grabs Benjamin. Benjamin tries to run away; Delilah grabs Benjamin and they have a tug-of-war with him. Eventually Caiaphas wins and drags Benjamin off screaming.

Delilah:	*(Calling off)* Come back you thug. Leave him alone. *(To herself)* What am I going to do? Now they've got Benjamin, they might do anything to him. I wonder if Jesus is really alive. Benjamin certainly thought so. But I must think of a way of rescuing Benjamin. *(Thinks for a moment)* Ah, I have a cunning plan that will expose that cruel creep Caiaphas at his weakest point. I shall reduce him to a phobic frenzy and in the heat of a reptile rampage we shall break Benjamin's bonds. But to make it work I shall need a super slippery, slithery snake. *(Exits)*

Enter Caiaphas dragging Benjamin.

Caiaphas:	Right! Now I've got you. I'm going to make you talk. *(Pushes Benjamin into a chair)* And if you say Jesus is alive again I'll have to deal seriously with you. I might even sing to you.
Benjamin:	Aaarggh, no! Not that!

Enter Delilah carrying a rubber snake.

Delilah:	*(Aside)* OK, Caiaphas. Your game's over. *(Throws a rubber snake at Caiaphas's neck and shouts)* Snake!
Caiaphas:	Aaarggh! *(Grabs at the snake and has a violent struggle with it. In the course of his struggling he staggers off stage)*
Delilah:	Are you all right?
Benjamin:	Yeah. Thanks, Delilah. I thought I was done for there. Hey! We'd better go, or we're going to be late.
Delilah:	What for? Are we going to see Jesus?
Benjamin:	I don't know. But, unless we hurry, we're going to miss the start of the camel race. *(Runs off)*
Delilah:	*(To the audience)* Typical! *(Runs after him)*

EASTER SUNDAY EVENING

Dramatic reading

'The King comes to his own' from Dorothy Sayers' plays *The Man Born to be King* can be a very powerful and moving presentation. Try it in the style of a radio play with voices only but with music and sound effects. Plan well in advance and experiment with lighting and sound. If you decide that the readers will not be visible, make sure there is something visual at the front of the church to act as a focal point. A large candle, banner or graphics on the OHP would be most helpful. Permission must be obtained for this play. Write to the International Copyright Bureau, 22a Aubery House, Maida Avenue, London W2 1TQ (tel: 071 724 8034). A small fee will be charged.

Easter carol service

Base this service on the familiar Christmas pattern. Use Easter readings, hymns and songs. You could go back over some of the events of Holy Week or simply start with the actual death and burial of Jesus and then go on to some of the resurrection appearances (Matthew 27:62-66; Matthew 28:2-4; Luke 24:1-9,11; Luke 24:13-35,36-49; John 19:28-30,38-42; John 20:11-18). If you adapt this for the first Sunday after Easter, then use the appearances of the first eight days. Appropriate readings from the epistles can be very helpful (Romans 1:1-4; Romans 6:3-14; Acts 2:22-36; verses from 1 Corinthians 15). Use 1 Peter 1:3-5 and Romans 6:9-11 as a New Testament psalm.

Meditation

Hymn: 'Jesus Christ is risen today'

Introduction: In this service, we are going to read and meditate upon the four encounters with the risen Lord Jesus, as recorded in St John's Gospel. We shall look at the time, the place and the state of mind of the people to whom Jesus appeared, and consider how we too might experience his living presence in our lives.

First reading: Jesus appears to Mary Magdalene (John 20:1-18)

Meditation: (script on page 43) – followed by silence

Hymn: 'O love that will not let me go'

Second reading:	Jesus appears to ten disciples (John 20:19-23)
Meditation:	(script on page 44) – followed by silence
Hymn:	'The strife is o'er, the battle done'
Third reading:	Jesus and Thomas (John 20:24-29)
Meditation:	(script on page 45) – followed by silence
Hymn:	'I know that my redeemer lives'
Fourth reading:	Seven disciples out fishing meet Jesus again (John 21:1-19)
Meditation:	(script on page 45) – followed by silence
Final reading and conclusion:	John 20:29 and 21:25
Hymn:	'Thine be the glory' – followed by the Blessing

MEDITATIONS

Mary Magdalene (John 20:1-18)

The time is very early in the morning, while it is still dark. Mary, a woman with a chequered past, has found healing, love and acceptance since Jesus cast out seven demons from her. From then on, devoted to him, she has followed him and provided for his needs. Unlike most of the disciples, she has followed Jesus to the bitter end, to the cross and to the tomb, watching till all hope seems extinguished.

And yet, after two sleepless nights and a long sabbath day of grieving, Mary does not give up. She comes very early on Sunday morning while it is still dark – dark within her heart as well as without – to see how she might still express her love for her Lord.

To find Jesus for ourselves, we need to come alone, quietly and privately, to read his word and pray, opening our minds to the possibility that he is indeed alive and will speak to us.

The place of encounter for Mary was the garden. Gardens at springtime speak to us of life after death, light after darkness.

Mary Magdalene was in deep distress and weeping. How many of us over the years have found Jesus in times of grief and heartbreak, times when there is no human answer of comfort or healing. Jesus came and called Mary by name, and she knew again his undying love.

Take the words of the prophet Isaiah for yourself:

'Do not be afraid – I will save you.
I have called you by name – you are mine.
When you pass through deep waters I will be with you.
You are precious to me. I love you and give you honour.'

Imagine yourself walking slowly into that shadowy, tree-lined garden.

It is dark, but gradually the sky turns red and then gold. The sun rises, and in a shaft of sunlight between two olive trees you see a figure coming towards you.

He calls your name... and you know it is the Lord. You hurry towards him and kneel at his feet.

He says, 'You are precious in my sight and I love you.'

Now tell him all your sorrows, and your failures, and your disappointments.

He will understand.

Ten disciples
(John 20:19-23)

It is now the end of that momentous day. The disciples are gathered together, and guess what they are discussing! Surely, about the time they have spent with Jesus, hearing his wonderful words, watching his miraculous actions, learning to pray like him, learning to heal and cast out demons, coming to realize who Jesus is: in Peter's words, the Christ, the Son of the living God.

But now – it seems that the Jewish and Roman authorities have had the last word, even over the Son of God. If they could get rid of Jesus the Christ, what might they do to his accomplices?

It's at the end of the day, when we reflect on events and try to puzzle out their significance, that anxiety, even fear, can grip our imagination and test our faith.

The disciples are together in a closed room, behind locked doors: a place of fear, tension and disappointment, perhaps anger and recrimination. At times like this, when the opposition to us as Christians seems overwhelming, we put up barriers against the world. We seek to protect ourselves by gathering in a holy huddle with like-minded people, reliving the past, sharing our fear and bewilderment.

But even now, Jesus can break through to bring peace and joy. However threatened and beleaguered we may feel, Jesus can be with us to say, 'Peace be with you.'

He shows the disciples his hands and side, the wounds he has suffered and borne and has overcome by the power of God. And they have peace and joy that, as he has overcome, so might they, whatever the suffering ahead.

Jesus breathes his Spirit into them, empowering them to come out from their locked and barred sanctum, and go into that threatening world taking his message of forgiveness and joy.

In your imagination climb the stone steps to that upper room. Bolt the door behind you, and draw the blinds so that no one can see you except God, your heavenly Father who loves you. Tell him now of what or of whom you are afraid. Realize that others around you are afraid, too.

Now someone is lighting the lamp. He calls your name...

In the dim light you see the scars in his hands, and you know it is Jesus. You remember his fear, sweating drops of blood in the garden of Gethsemane. His worst fears were realized on the cross.

But God has brought him through, victorious.

He says to you, 'When you pass through deep waters, I will be with you. Your troubles will not overwhelm you.'

He breathes his Spirit upon you, and you feel the warmth of his peace and joy.

Jesus and Thomas (John 20:24-29)

Much human acclamation greets those who are first in their field – the first conquerors of Everest, the first to transplant a human heart, the first test-tube baby, the first female astronaut. But in God's kingdom, the first will be last, and the last first. Thomas is the last disciple to see the risen Christ, but when he does, he finds a convincing, first-hand faith. God's timing is not ours, but his is always perfect.

The time is a week later. It is evening and again the followers of Jesus are together, behind closed doors. Thomas is surrounded by believers, witnesses of the resurrection, but their faith is still too weak to meet openly in public. Thomas himself is full of doubts, in spite of his friends' testimony and arguments. He cannot accept that Jesus is alive until he sees for himself.

Maybe you have been coming to church for some time, weeks or even years. You've heard many sermons, many arguments, but Jesus isn't yet real and alive for you. Then look at Thomas! How much better to be honest about your doubts than to profess an insincere faith! Yet Thomas was open and ready to accept the evidence when he could see it for himself. Then he was humble enough to kneel and worship – 'My Lord and my God.'

If you don't believe, what's stopping you? Are you, like Thomas, wanting to believe, seeking honest answers and prepared to accept them? If so, you must stay with the company of believers and keep asking questions until you get your answers.

Or are you like the Pharisees who asked for a sign, a miracle, before they would believe? They were putting off the moment of acknowledging Jesus for who, deep down, they knew he was.

'Blessed are those who have not seen and yet believe,' said Jesus.

Remember the steps you climbed in your imagination? Go up them again. Bolt the door. Draw the blinds.

Someone is lighting a lamp.

He gives a familiar greeting in a familiar voice: 'Peace be with you.' He greets you by name.

Tell him your doubts. Ask him your questions. Now look at his nail-scarred hands and feet.

If you now believe he is alive, bow down and worship him.

If not, maybe he wants you to ask someone stronger in faith for help. Perhaps he is saying, 'The time is not right for you yet. You will understand in my good time.'

Jesus says: 'I will ask the Father and he will give you another helper who will stay with you for ever. He is the Spirit who reveals the truth about God. Seek and you will find. Ask and you will receive.'

Seven disciples out fishing (John 21:1-19)

The time is now sunrise, after a fruitless (or should it be fishless?) night's fishing. It is 'some time later' – we don't know how long – but apparently disciples who have seen Jesus alive still need to encounter him again to receive further proof and encouragement.

The place is by the shore of Lake Galilee, the place where Jesus had told them to meet him, the place of powerful memories of being with Jesus, hearing his teaching, experiencing his power over diseased minds and bodies, over loaves and fishes, over wind and waves, even over empty fishing nets.

How are the disciples feeling? Flat? Fed up? Frustrated? Impatient for a revival of the 'good old days' when crowds came to Jesus? They've come down to earth with a bump after the first exciting experience of the resurrection.

Perhaps some of us feel like that, in our own discipleship, or in the state of our church or fellowship.

But as the disciples get on with their everyday tasks, Jesus appears to them again. He reminds them of his power in the past by giving them a huge catch of fish, showing them that his love and power are still the same even though he may be out of sight.

Jesus speaks to Simon Peter especially, the disheartened leader of the group, still grieving over his triple denial of Jesus. Jesus challenges him to a new start, recalling the first challenge to 'follow me', and gives him a new task of feeding the lambs, the little ones in the faith.

The first moment of recognition of the living Lord is not the last. It must lead to a lifetime of worship and loving service, in which Jesus from time to time will encourage us by new highlights of recognition and re-commissioning, perhaps to new forms of service.

To those of us who have seen Jesus and believe in him, he says, 'Keep on loving me, keep on following me, keep on feeding my lambs, keep on bringing glory to God's name.'

You are in a fishing boat on the Sea of Galilee as the sun is rising in a clear blue sky.

Hear the water lapping against the wooden boat. Feel the crunch as the boat reaches the beach.

Search your memory for times when Jesus has been with you in a powerful way. Now climb over the side into cold, shallow water. Drag your tired limbs and breaking nets up the shingly beach. You can smell woodsmoke and the appetizing smell of fresh fish being cooked.

You see Jesus there, providing for your needs – just what you wanted! Together you enjoy a wonderful breakfast.

Then Jesus looks you straight in the eye, and you glimpse the scars of a crown of thorns on his brow. He calls you by name. 'Do you love me?'

If your answer is, 'Yes Lord, you know that I love you,' ask him what he wants you to do for him.

If you cannot yet answer, 'Yes, Lord, I love you,' picture Jesus on the cross, suffering and dying not for his own sin, but for yours. Then see him here, alive again, offering you the forgiveness he has won for you. Confess your sin, believe and trust in him, and ask him to be Lord of your life.

May our Lord reveal himself to each one of us, transforming our lives by his constant presence with us, now and for evermore.

EASTER MONDAY

Easter party or picnic

Choose a theme which gives a good link to the Easter biblical narratives. Plan well in advance and involve others in the preparation. Food, games, activities and decorations should follow the theme. Singing and a talk can be included. Use secular as well as spiritual material.

Fishing party

John 21 is the biblical story. Barbecued fish is excellent – and what an excuse for chips! This can be adapted for the sea or the beach or boats. Include fishing games and activities.

Footsteps party

It can be exciting to follow Jesus in and out of Jerusalem during Holy Week – from the Eastern Gate to the temple, out to Bethany, back to the upper room, out to the garden of Gethsemane, to the High Priest's palace and Pilate's house, to Calvary and to the garden tomb, then back to the upper room and the Sea of Galilee. A plan could be made of the city of Jerusalem, or even a model built in the church hall. Styles of transport, food for the journey, and games can be fitted into the theme.

Surprise party

The life of Jesus, especially his last week on earth, held lots of surprises. This calls for surprise food and games. Take any of the resurrection appearances which caused the disciples to be surprised. If the box of helium balloons hasn't been used at the Easter Sunday service, it could be used here. Write 'Alleluia' on cards and attach them to the tails of helium balloons. Then put the balloons in the biggest box you can find and at an appropriate point release them. They'll float skywards and stay up for weeks.

Easter adventure week

You may like to follow an Easter theme for this and look at some of the appearances of Jesus to his disciples. You could look at characters who were dramatically changed by the resurrection (for example, Peter). The fishing/boat/sea theme could be developed; there are many stories in the life of Christ to do with this.

Have appropriate games, songs and activities. You could make a scrapbook or produce a newspaper, such as the *Jerusalem Journal* or the *Galilean Gazette*. Gathering together material to use in the family service on the Sunday after Easter can be a very rewarding, if demanding, exercise.

■ Reference booklist

Further resources from CPAS

1994 CPAS Code	Title	Author and Publisher
02151/2	Church Family Worship	Hodder and Stoughton
03418	For All the Family	Michael Botting, Kingsway
03483	More for All the Family	Michael Botting, Kingsway
03547	Drama for All the Family	Michael Botting, Kingsway
03125/6	Prayers for the People	HarperCollins

Other books

Lent, Holy Week and Easter	SPCK
Patterns of Worship	Church House Publishing

Banner-making books

An Army with Banners	Miss Priscilla Nunnerly, 9 Chestnut Court,
Banners in His Name	Chestnut Lane, Amersham, Bucks HP6 6ED
Banner Makers to the King	

■ Acknowledgements

A considerable number of people have contributed to this book. Virtually all are active in local church leadership. We thank them for offering their materials and especially for the editorial work done by Pam Harvey, Morris Rodham, Douglas Drye and John Moore.

Lent: *Longings*, David Hopwood

Mothering Sunday: *A family in need, Togetherness* adapted from Scripture Union's *Learning All Together* and used by kind permission. *Neville and Toad, Abraham and Sarah, From a Son*, David Hopwood

Palm Sunday: *Meditation*, David Hopwood

Maundy Thursday: *Timberman*, David Hopwood; *These Hands*, Alan Boddington

Good Friday: *Simon the Crossbearer*, Janice Newton; *Hands*, David Hopwood

Easter: Banners, Rachel McHugh

Copyright © 1994

Published by
CPAS
Athena Drive
Tachbrook Park
WARWICK
CV34 6NG

Telephone: (01926) 334242
Orderline: (01926) 335855

Church Pastoral Aid Society
Registered Charity No 1007820
A company limited by guarantee

First Edition 1994
Reprinted 1996
ISBN 0 9077 50524

All rights reserved. Permission is given for purchasers to copy the illustrations on to acetates for sermons and talks provided the CPAS copyright notice is retained on each sheet.

British Library Cataloguing-in-Publication Data: A catalogue record for this book is available from the British Library.

Illustrations by Doug Hewitt

Editorial and Design by AD Publishing Services Ltd

Printed by Unigraph Printing Services, Sheffield